For King and Kingdom

Preparing for the Return of the King

For King and Kingdom

Copyright © 2017-2020
by Robert "B.J." Gardner Corbin Jr.
All rights reserved.
1st Edition (R3) Paperback
ISBN 978-1-71601-495-6

Edited by B.J. Corbin and Jennifer Corbin
Last edited: May 6, 2020

www.bjcorbin.com

Most biblical references via www.biblehub.com using the English Standard Version (ESV), unless noted.

Matthew 24:14

And this **gospel of the kingdom** will be proclaimed throughout the whole world as a testimony to all nations, and then the end will come.

As the world grows darker,
seek and long for the light…
prepare for the true King.

Contents

Preface

Introduction

A King Before Time Began

Abraham to King David to Jesus

Signs Before Coming Kingdom - Deception & Falling Away

The Third Jewish Temple

Return of King Jesus

Summary

Brief Testimony

How to Become a Christian

Appendix

Bibliography

Other Books by B.J. Corbin

Preface

There have been many "kingdoms" throughout human history, so what *kingdom* is being referenced in this book? The everlasting kingdom (heaven & earth) of the one true God, and His Son, as described in the Bible.

The ancient and modern name of the king:
יְהוֹשֻׁעַ Yehoshua (Hebrew)
יֵשׁוּעַ Yeshua (Hebrew/Aramaic)
Ἰησοῦς transliterated as
Iēsous… *ee-ay-sooce* (Greek)
Iesus (Latin)
Jesus (English)
Upon His return, He will have a name that only He knows.

Jesus likely spoke Jewish Palestinian Aramaic, a Western Aramaic language, and closely related to Hebrew.

The following are some Bible verses about the king and His kingdom.

Exodus 15:18
> 18 The LORD will reign forever and ever.

Psalm 145:11-13
> 11 They shall speak of the glory of **your kingdom**
> and tell of your power,
> 12 to make known to the children of man your mighty deeds, and the glorious splendor of your kingdom.
> 13 Your kingdom is an everlasting kingdom, and your dominion endures throughout all generations.

When Jesus was teaching His disciples how to pray, He included "**Your kingdom** come."

Matthew 6:9-10
> 9 Pray then like this:

"Our Father in heaven,
hallowed be your name
10 Your kingdom come,
your will be done,
on earth as it is in heaven.

This future kingdom, according to the Book of Revelation chapter 21, is comprised of a new heaven and new earth.

May our every thought and action be… *For King and Kingdom.*

Introduction

Most people, even people that do not believe in the Judeo-Christian God or His son, sense that this world is slipping into darkness and chaos. Not much of an "earthly kingdom" currently exists that one would admire. But it is this hope for peace that will usher in a coming world leader who is antichrist. The very involvement of this world leader with a seven year "peace" agreement including the nation of Israel, and possibility involving the rebuilding of the Jewish Temple, will begin the seven year tribulation mentioned in the Book of Daniel chapter 9. Some consider the second 3-1/2 years of this agreement period to be the *Great Tribulation*, a time of many judgments and calamities.

Biblical prophecy is pointing towards a coming kingdom, where the son of God, Jesus (Yeshua), is going to reign for a thousand years in a new heaven and a new earth, and a new Jerusalem. What's next after that is a mystery.

Prophecy is not so much about predicting the future or knowing *what's next* so we seem to possess insider information and appear clever. It's about the king and His kingdom.

While many Christians hope for and even predict a major revival of the church, the Bible says the church will become apostate or Laodicean, as described in the Book of Revelation. By allowing **deception**, many "believers" will fall away from the faith.

Matthew 24:10-14

> 10 And then many will **fall away** and betray one another and hate one another. 11 And many false prophets will arise and lead many astray. 12 And because lawlessness will be increased, the love of many will grow cold. 13 But the one who endures to the end will be saved. 14 And this **gospel of the kingdom** will be proclaimed throughout the whole world as a testimony to all nations, and then the end will come.

Don't be impressed (deceived) by the signs and wonders that will be performed by a coming world leader. The peace he will offer will be a false peace, and taking his name or 666 mark (*likely a small implanted electronic chip on the right hand or forehead*), will be required to buy or sell, but will lead to eternal damnation. **<u>DON'T</u> TAKE THE MARK!**

Suffice to say, it is best not to put your hope in a man or this world to bring a lasting peace, but the coming messiah, Jesus, who will reign as king in the new kingdom.

A King Before Time Began

Non-Christians often consider Jesus in a historical context, while Christians tend to think of Jesus as Savior for His sacrifice on the cross and resurrection… even as the coming future king. But how often to we think of Jesus as *pre-existent*? That Jesus existed before He was born, and always was… and always will be. For biblical prophecy to be so precise and accurate, we can surmise God is not constrained by "time" and can exist outside of our present dimension or reality.

John 17:5, 24
> 5 And now, Father, glorify me in your own presence with the glory that I had with you **before the world existed**.

> 24 Father, I desire that they also, whom you have given me, may be with me where I am, to see my glory that you have given me

because you loved me **before the foundation of the world**.

There are biblical scriptures of God telling His prophets, like Jeremiah, that they were "known" before being in their mother's womb.

Jeremiah 1:5
> "Before I formed you in the womb I knew you, and before you were born I consecrated you; I appointed you a prophet to the nations."

As mortal humans facing certain death and destined to return back to the dust (Genesis 3:19), we possess an eternal soul longing for a future heavenly body. (see my book *The Shining Suit*)

2 Corinthians 5:1
> For we know that if the tent that is our earthly home is destroyed, we have a building from

God, a house not made with hands, eternal in the heavens.

Since Jesus existed before the foundation of the world, this should provide comfort that in God's timing, Jesus will return and reign as the king of the new kingdom.

Abraham to King David to Jesus

God promises "post-Flood" Abraham that from his seed will come kings and an everlasting covenant.

Genesis 17:6-7
> 6 I will make you exceedingly fruitful, and I will make you into nations, and **kings shall come from you**. 7 And I will establish my covenant between me and you and your offspring after you throughout their generations for an everlasting covenant, to be God to you and to your offspring after you.

The line of kingship is restricted during the time of Jacob, to his son **Judah**.

Genesis 49:10
> The scepter shall not depart from Judah, nor the ruler's staff from between his feet, until tribute comes to him; and to him shall be the obedience of the peoples.

In 1 Chronicles 17:14, 2 Samuel 7:16, and Psalm 89:3-4, the throne of the king is further restricted to the line of **David**.

Psalm 89:3-4
> 3 You have said, "I have made a covenant with my chosen one;
> I have sworn to David my servant:
> 4 'I will establish your offspring forever,
> and **build your throne** for all generations.'"
> Selah

David's son, Solomon, becomes king and builds the first temple. Approximately 927 years after the death of King Solomon, Jesus (from the line of David) is born to the virgin Mary in the town of Bethlehem.

The angel Gabriel was sent by God to inform Mary about the special child she would conceive and deliver.

Luke 1:31-33
> 31 And behold, you will conceive in your womb and bear a son, and you shall call his name Jesus. 32 He will be great and will be called the Son of the Most High. **And the Lord God will give to him the throne of his father David, 33 and he will reign over the house of Jacob forever, and of his kingdom there will be no end.**"

Jesus grew up and performed many miracles, and preached of repentance and the kingdom of God.

Matthew 4:17 ESV
> 17 From that time Jesus began to preach, saying, "Repent, for the **kingdom** of heaven is at hand."

Many people were expecting a Messiah to end the rule of Rome, but it was the sacrifice for all sins that was provided, once and for all. Jesus' first coming would be as a suffering servant, described in the Book of Isaiah chapter 53. In Revelation 19, it describes Jesus returning as the *King of kings*.

Revelation 19:11-16
> 11 Then I saw heaven opened, and behold, a white horse! The one sitting on it is called **Faithful and True**, and in righteousness he judges and makes war. 12 His eyes are like a flame of fire, and on his head are many diadems, and he has a name written that no one knows but himself. 13 He is clothed in a robe dipped in blood, and the name by which he is called is **The Word of God**. 14 And the armies of heaven, arrayed in fine linen, white and pure, were following him on white horses. 15 From his mouth comes a sharp sword with which to strike down the nations, and he will rule them with a rod of iron. He will tread the winepress of the fury of the wrath of God the Almighty. 16 On his robe and on his thigh he has a name written, **King of kings** and **Lord of lords**.

Jesus is destined to return and be the *King of kings* and the *Lord of lords*. With all the chaos and confusion in this world, one must be diligent in the work of the coming kingdom to avoid becoming distracted.

Signs Before Coming Kingdom
Deception & Falling Away

Before Jesus returns as king of the new heaven, the new earth, and the new Jerusalem, the Bible predicts a great apostasy or falling away. The love of many will grow cold and leave the church.

1 Timothy 4:1-5

> 1 Now the Spirit expressly says that in later times **some will depart from the faith** by devoting themselves to deceitful spirits and teachings of demons, 2 through the insincerity of liars whose consciences are seared, 3 who forbid marriage and require abstinence from foods that God created to be received with thanksgiving by those who believe and know the truth. 4 For everything created by God is good, and nothing is to be rejected if it is received with thanksgiving, 5 for it is made holy by the word of God and prayer.

Knowing this, one must carefully consider the church they attend. Is the leadership of the church theologically sound?

The Third Jewish Temple

We anticipate the construction of a Third Temple in Jerusalem to fulfill biblical prophecy, Daniel 9:27, the abomination of desolation. This is where a world leader (antichrist) sits in the temple as a god. The building of the temple will likely be a key component of the future seven year "peace" agreement including Israel. Instead of peace, this will be considered a time of great tribulation and judgments.

There are several organizations dedicated to the construction of a Third Jewish Temple.

The Temple Institute
templeinstitute.org

Temple Mount and Eretz Yisrael Faithful Movement

templemountfaithful.org

The following picture shows a model of the proposed Third Jewish Temple.

Image Source: http://www.jta.org/wp-content/uploads/2013/07/Second-Temple.jpg

The prophet Ezekiel received a vision of the future temple as described in the book of Ezekiel chapters 40-48.

The first Jewish temple was built around 957 BC during the time of Solomon, son of King David.

After the Jews were released from Babylonian captivity by Persian King Cyrus, the Second Temple is restored around 515 BC, but lacking the Ark of the Covenant, prophecy and the spiritual power demonstrated during the First Temple period.

Antiochus IV Epiphanes, a Greek king (175-164 BC), desecrated the Second Temple by installing a statue of Zeus and sacrificing pigs. Many biblical scholars consider this incident a forerunner to the predicted antichrist *abomination of desolation* event occurring midway during the seven year tribulation, mentioned in the Book of Daniel 9:27, 11:31 and 12:11.

The Second Temple was expanded during the reign of Herod the Great, a Roman king from 37-4 BC. We read in the Gospels Jesus predicted that temple would be destroyed:

Matthew 24:1-2

> 1 Jesus left the temple and was going away, when his disciples came to point out to him the buildings of the temple. 2 But he answered them, "You see all these, do you not? Truly, I say to you, there will not be left here one stone upon another that will not be thrown down."

Mark 13:1-2

> 1 And as he came out of the temple, one of his disciples said to him, "Look, Teacher, what wonderful stones and what wonderful buildings!" 2 And Jesus said to him, "Do you see these great buildings? There will not be left here one stone upon another that will not be thrown down."

In 70 AD, the Second Temple, as Jesus predicted, was completely destroyed. The siege and destruction of Jerusalem was led by the Roman leader named Titus.

God's Future Temple

The Book of Revelation in chapter 21, describes the future kingdom of God as Jesus ruling with no temple.

Revelation 21:22-23

> 22 And I saw **no temple in the city**, for its temple is the Lord God the Almighty and the Lamb. 23 And the city has no need of sun or moon to shine on it, for the glory of God gives it light, and its lamp is the Lamb.

The coming kingdom will be lit by the light of the Lamb who was slain. Come Lord Jesus!

Return of King Jesus

Jesus came to earth the first time as a suffering servant, but will return as a mighty king.

Many Christian scholars associate the Jewish spring feasts with the first coming of Jesus (suffering servant), and the fall feasts with the second coming of Jesus (king).

The three pilgrimage festivals are Pesach (Passover), Shavuot (Weeks or Pentecost), and Sukkot (Tabernacles, Tents or Booths)

The following tables review the spring and fall Jewish feasts from a Christian perspective.

Spring Feasts	Date	Christian View

Pesach (Passover) Sedar meal with lamb, matzo bread, wine	Nisan 14 (March/April) Exodus 12	Crucification of Jesus
Unleavened Bread (Hag HaMatzah)	Nisan 15	Jesus Burial
First Fruits (barley harvest) Bikkurim	Nisan 17	Jesus Resurrection
Shavuot (pronounced shah-voo-oat) first fruits wheat harvest "wave offering" of two loaves of leavened bread, the Feast of Weeks, Pentecost	50 days (a week of weeks) after Passover Sivan 6 (May/June) Moses receives the Law, David born and died.	Holy Spirit, speak in other tongues Acts 2

*** Church Age ***

Fall Feasts	Date	Christian View
Trumpets (Yom Teruah or Rosh HaShanah)	Tishrei 1	Rapture

Day of Atonement (Yom Kippur)	Tishrei 10	Armageddon and Jesus 2nd Coming
Sukkot or the Feast of Tabernacles (Tents or Booths) gathering/end of the harvest	Tishrei 15 (Sept/Oct) Wave lulav & etrog	Millennium, God lives with man like in the Garden of Eden.

Though many people make a parallel between the Feast of Trumpets and the Rapture, we are reminded in the Book of Matthew chapter 24, that no one knows the day, except the Father God.

Matthew 24:36
> 36 "But concerning that day and hour **no one knows**, not even the angels of heaven, nor the Son but the Father only.

Probably the best advice, would be to live each day for the kingdom and long for the return of the king.

Gaining Entrance to the Kingdom
Christ Came to Fulfill the Law

Some are under the impression that by being under the new covenant or biblical New Testament, we have the grace and forgiveness of Jesus. That this is somehow easier than trying to follow laws (being legalistic). In fact, as you read some of the Bible verses below, Jesus, by including the intent of the heart, made His commandments harder to follow, not easier.

Matthew 5:17-20

> 17 "Do not think that I have come to abolish the Law or the Prophets; I have not come to abolish them but to fulfill them. 18 For truly, I say to you, until heaven and earth pass away, not an iota, not a dot, will pass from the Law until all is accomplished. 19 Therefore whoever relaxes one of the least of these commandments and teaches others to do the same will be called least in the kingdom of

heaven, but whoever does them and teaches them will be called great in the kingdom of heaven. 20 For I tell you, unless your righteousness exceeds that of the scribes and Pharisees, you will never enter the kingdom of heaven.

1 John 5:2-3

2 By this we know that we love the children of God, when we love God and obey his commandments. 3 For this is the love of God, that we keep his commandments. And his commandments are not burdensome.

Revelation 21:1-8 ESV

1 Then I saw a new heaven and a new earth, for the first heaven and the first earth had passed away, and the sea was no more. 2 And I saw the holy city, new Jerusalem, coming down out of heaven from God, prepared as a bride adorned for her husband. 3 And I heard a loud voice from the throne saying, "Behold, the dwelling place of God is with man. He will dwell with them, and they will be his people, and God himself will be

with them as their God. 4 He will wipe away every tear from their eyes, and death shall be no more, neither shall there be mourning, nor crying, nor pain anymore, for the former things have passed away."

5 And he who was seated on the throne said, "Behold, I am making all things new." Also he said, "Write this down, for these words are trustworthy and true." 6 And he said to me, "It is done! I am the Alpha and the Omega, the beginning and the end. To the thirsty I will give from the spring of the water of life without payment. 7 **The one who conquers will have this heritage, and I will be his God and he will be my son.** 8 But as for the cowardly, the faithless, the detestable, as for murderers, the sexually immoral, sorcerers, idolaters, and all liars, their portion will be in the lake that burns with fire and sulfur, which is the second death."

May God grant us the grace to be conquerers, to be brave and pure of heart, that we will be called sons of God. Blessed are those glad at the appearing of our Lord and Savior, Jesus, and granted access to the Tree of Life.

Summary

The following scripture in the Book of Matthew chapter 24 sums up the purpose and focus of this book.

Matthew 24:14 (ESV)
> 14 And this **gospel of the kingdom** will be proclaimed throughout the whole world as a testimony to all nations, and then the end will come.

Many Christians will say… I am not sure of my "calling." As in not sure what God wants me to do with my life. If you are a Christian, one of your primary tasks according to the Bible, is to **proclaim the coming kingdom**. That is, to preach and promote the return of Jesus Christ, the Messiah (anointed one), as King of kings and Lord of lords.

If you are not a Christian, you first need to get yourself in right relationship with God. Please read the section near the end of this book titled… *How to Become a Christian.*

I hope this book has been a reminder that the king is coming, and we should be mindful on that certainty every minute of every day.

For King and Kingdom

Brief Testimony

A testimony, in the biblical sense, is sharing your story of how you became a follower of God and His son, *Jesus* (Yeshua in the Hebrew language).

I was raised by great Christian parents who worked hard and made their children attend church. Our father had an interest in biblical prophecy, especially as it related to the nation of Israel.

While a teenager in high school, a friend invited me to attend a revival in Chincoteague, Virginia. As I sat listening to a "fire and brimstone" preacher, I felt the heavy weight of my sins, and was convicted by the Holy Spirit of my past mistakes and transgressions. I recall holding onto the folding, metal chair to keep from going forward during the altar call. An altar call is when you are invited to come to front of the church or meeting to confess your sins publicly and accept Jesus as your Lord and Savior. I did not go forward that night, but it was clear the Holy Spirit was working *in me*… or *on me* for months after the revival.

One cool night in downtown Pocomoke City, a classmate and fellow soccer team member named Steve, led me to the Lord. We drove with some others to the soccer field, and prayed to accept Jesus as Lord.

After attending First Baptist Church for several months, I made a public declaration of my faith in Jesus and was water baptized… in the name of the Father, the Son, and the Holy Spirit.

If you have read this book and have not made your own personal commitment to follow Jesus, ask the Holy Spirit to reveal your sins and need of a Savior. Humble yourself before God and tell Him you are *deeply sorry* for your sins, ask for forgiveness, and accept salvation by believing in His son, Jesus, who was beaten, shed His blood on a cross, and died for mankind's sins. The best part is that by believing in Jesus, you also share in the *blessed hope*, that we will one day rise to meet Jesus in the clouds.

Consider the following Bible verses:

John 3:16 NASB

> 16 For God so loved the world, that He gave His only begotten Son, that whoever believes in Him shall not perish, but have eternal life.

John 14:6 NASB

> 6 Jesus said to him, "I am the way, and the truth, and the life; no one comes to the Father but through Me.

Romans 6:23 NASB

> 23 For the wages of sin is death, but the free gift of God is eternal life in Christ Jesus our Lord.

Romans 10:9-10 NASB

> 9 that if you confess with your mouth Jesus as Lord, and believe in your heart that God raised Him from the dead, you will be saved; 10 for with the heart a person believes, resulting in righteousness, and with the mouth he confesses, resulting in salvation.

How to Become a Christian

* *Repent of your sins*

You may or may not have heard about Moses

and the *Ten Commandments*. Below is a condensed version of Exodus 20:1-17.

1) I am the LORD thy God, Thou Shalt Have No Other Gods Beside Me
2) Thou Shalt Not Worship Any Graven Images
3) Thou Shalt Not Take the Name of the Lord Thy God in Vain
4) Remember the Sabbath Day to Rest and Keep it Holy
5) Honor Thy Father and Thy Mother
6) Thou Shalt Not Kill
7) Thou Shalt Not Commit Adultery
8) Thou Shalt Not Steal
9) Thou Shalt Not Bear False Witness
10) Thou Shalt Not Covet Anything That is Thy Neighbor's

Jesus summed up the Ten Commandments into just two:

Matthew 22:37-40 NASB

> 37 And He said to him, " 'YOU SHALL LOVE THE LORD YOUR GOD WITH ALL YOUR HEART, AND WITH ALL YOUR SOUL, AND WITH ALL YOUR MIND.' 38 "This is the great and foremost commandment. 39 "The second is like it, 'YOU SHALL LOVE YOUR NEIGHBOR AS YOURSELF.' 40 "On these

two commandments depend the whole Law and the Prophets."

Simply put… *love God… love others.*

These are laws that all men and women break at some point in their lives. Whether or not you have read and know these laws, you still *know* them in your heart from a young age. Jesus, in His teaching, went beyond the "letter of the law" and included the *intent of the heart.* For example, in Matthew 5:27-28, Jesus said, *27" You have heard that it was said, 'YOU SHALL NOT COMMIT ADULTERY'; 28 but I say to you that everyone who looks at a woman with lust for her has already committed adultery with her in his heart."*

You need to verbally and publicly acknowledge the things you have done wrong (sin), and be deeply sorry, and turn away from your sins (repent).

*** Confess Jesus, the son of God, as your Lord and Savior**

Jesus is the only one able to forgive your sins. By His shed-blood sacrifice on the cross at Calvary and His resurrection from the dead three days later, He paid the debt of sin once and for all. Our hope is, that we too, will one day be resurrected and meet Jesus in the clouds upon His return.

*** Get water baptized**

Following Jesus' example of being water baptized. Have a pastor, preacher or believer immerse your body in water declaring… in the name of the Father, the Son, and the Holy Spirit.

Acts 2:38 NASB

> Peter said to them, "**Repent**, and each of you be **baptized** in the name of Jesus Christ for the forgiveness of your sins; and you will receive the gift of the Holy Spirit."

Next Steps

- Be guided by the Holy Spirit
- Study the Bible
- Join a body of Christian believers
- Seek, trust and obey God

Discover your gifts and use your talents for the purpose of God's Kingdom… until Jesus returns!

THE KINGDOM IS HERE… BUT NOT YET! The resurrection of Jesus has set in motion future events that will usher in the new coming kingdom.

Bibliography

Corbin, B.J. (2017). Prophetic Forecast
ISBN 978-1-387-18394-4

Corbin, B.J. (2017). Learn the Bible in 1 Hour
ISBN 978-1-387-29448-0

The ESV® Bible (The Holy Bible, English Standard Version®) copyright © 2001 by Crossway Bibles, a publishing ministry of Good News Publishers.

Other Books by B.J. Corbin

The Explorers of Ararat: And the Search for Noah's Ark
Compilation of Ark researchers focused on Mt. Ararat.

Seven Mountains to Aratta
Explores the possible nexus between the Biblical mountains of Ararat and Sumerian Aratta.

Man from Modest Town
A family history and tribute.

The Shining Suit
Looks at the heavenly body angels "wear" and the future habitation we aspire to obtain.

Adams's Coat

Explores the *Book of Jasher* account of Adam's Coat being passed down many generations, even after the Flood.

Flood Before Fire
Based on Adam's prediction that the world would be destroyed by water and fire.

Prophetic Forecast
A summary of predicted future events.

Close Encounters with a Faraway God
A chronicle of people that had direct contact with God.

Learn the Bible in 1 Hour
A summary of the Bible intended to be a primer for further biblical study.

www.bjcorbin.com

www.ingramcontent.com/pod-product-compliance
Lightning Source LLC
Chambersburg PA
CBHW020023050426
42450CB00005B/624